Ruth

FIELDS OF GRACE

KRISTIN SCHMUCKER

Study Suggestions

We believe that the Bible is true, trustworthy, and timeless and that it is vitally important for all believers. These study suggestions are intended to help you more effectively study Scripture as you seek to know and love God through His Word.

SUGGESTED STUDY TOOLS

- A Bible

- A double-spaced, printed copy of the Scripture passages that this study covers. You can use a website like *www.biblegateway.com* to copy the text of a passage and print out a double-spaced copy to be able to mark on easily.

- A journal to write notes or prayers

- Pens, colored pencils, and highlighters

- A dictionary to look up unfamiliar words

HOW TO USE THIS STUDY

Begin your study time in prayer. Ask God to reveal Himself to you, to help you understand what you are reading, and to transform you with His Word (Psalm 119:18).

Before you read what is written in each day of the study itself, read the assigned passages of Scripture for that day. Use your double-spaced copy to circle, underline, highlight, draw arrows, and mark in any way you would like to help you dig deeper as you work through a passage.

Read the daily written content provided for the current study day.

Answer the questions that appear at the end of each study day.

HOW TO STUDY THE BIBLE

The inductive method provides tools for deeper and more intentional Bible study. To study a book of the Bible inductively, work through the steps below after reading background information on the book.

1

OBSERVATION & COMPREHENSION
Key question: What does the text say?

After reading the book of the Bible in its entirety at least once, begin working with smaller portions of the book. Read a passage of Scripture repetitively, and then mark the following items in the text:

- Key or repeated words and ideas
- Key themes
- Transition words (*Ex: therefore, but, because, if/then, likewise, etc.*)
- Lists
- Comparisons & Contrasts
- Commands
- Unfamiliar words (look these up in a dictionary)
- Questions you have about the text

2

INTERPRETATION
Key question: What does the text mean?

Once you have annotated the text, work through the following steps to help you interpret its meaning:

- Read the passage in other versions for a better understanding of the text.
- Read cross-references to help interpret Scripture with Scripture.
- Paraphrase or summarize the passage to check for understanding.
- Identify how the text reflects the metanarrative of Scripture, which is the story of creation, fall, redemption, and restoration.
- Read trustworthy commentaries if you need further insight into the meaning of the passage.

3 **APPLICATION**
Key Question: How should the truth of this passage change me?

Bible study is not merely an intellectual pursuit. The truths about God, ourselves, and the gospel that we discover in Scripture should produce transformation in our hearts and lives. Answer the following questions as you consider what you have learned in your study:

- What attributes of God's character are revealed in the passage?

  Consider places where the text directly states the character of God, as well as how His character is revealed through His words and actions.

- What do I learn about myself in light of who God is?

  Consider how you fall short of God's character, how the text reveals your sin nature, and what it says about your new identity in Christ.

- How should this truth change me?

  A passage of Scripture may contain direct commands telling us what to do or warnings about sins to avoid in order to help us grow in holiness. Other times our application flows out of seeing ourselves in light of God's character. As we pray and reflect on how God is calling us to change in light of His Word, we should be asking questions like, "How should I pray for God to change my heart?" and "What practical steps can I take toward cultivating habits of holiness?"

ATTRIBUTES OF GOD

ETERNAL

God has no beginning and no end. He always was, always is, and always will be.

HAB. 1:12 / REV. 1:8 / IS. 41:4

FAITHFUL

God is incapable of anything but fidelity. He is loyally devoted to His plan and purpose.

2 TIM. 2:13 / DEUT. 7:9
HEB. 10:23

GLORIOUS

God is ultimately beautiful, deserving of all praise and honor.

REV. 19:1 / PS. 104:1
EX. 40:34-35

GOOD

God is pure; there is no defilement in Him. He is unable to sin, and all He does is good.

GEN. 1:31 / PS. 34:8 / PS. 107:1

GRACIOUS

God is kind, giving to us gifts and benefits which we do not deserve.

2 KINGS 13:23 / PS. 145:8
IS. 30:18

HOLY

God is undefiled and unable to be in the presence of defilement. He is sacred and set-apart.

REV. 4:8 / LEV. 19:2 / HAB. 1:13

IMMUTABLE

God does not change. He is the same yesterday, today, and tomorrow.

1 SAM. 15:29 / ROM. 11:29
JAMES 1:17

JEALOUS

God is desirous of receiving the praise and affection He rightly deserves.

EX. 20:5 / DEUT. 4:23-24
JOSH. 24:19

JUST

God governs in perfect justice. He acts in accordance with justice. In Him there is no wrongdoing or dishonesty.

IS. 61:8 / DEUT. 32:4 / PS. 146:7-9

LOVE

God is eternally, enduringly, steadfastly loving and affectionate. He does not forsake or betray His covenant love.

JN. 3:16 / EPH. 2:4-5 / 1 JN. 4:16

MERCIFUL

God is compassionate, withholding us from the wrath that we deserve.

TITUS 3:5 / PS. 25:10
LAM. 3:22-23

OMNIPOTENT

God is all-powerful; His strength is unlimited.

MAT. 19:26 / JOB 42:1-2
JER. 32:27

OMNIPRESENT

God is everywhere; His presence is near and permeating.

PROV. 15:3 / PS. 139:7-10
JER. 23:23-24

OMNISCIENT

God is all-knowing; there is nothing unknown to Him.

PS. 147:4 / I JN. 3:20
HEB. 4:13

PATIENT

God is long-suffering and enduring. He gives ample opportunity for people to turn toward Him.

ROM. 2:4 / 2 PET. 3:9 / PS. 86:15

RIGHTEOUS

God is blameless and upright. There is no wrong found in Him.

PS. 119:137 / JER. 12:1
REV. 15:3

SOVEREIGN

God governs over all things; He is in complete control.

COL. 1:17 / PS. 24:1-2
1 CHRON. 29:11-12

TRUE

God is our measurement of what is fact. By Him are we able to discern true and false.

JN. 3:33 / ROM. 1:25 / JN. 14:6

WISE

God is infinitely knowledgeable and is judicious with His knowledge.

IS. 46:9-10 / IS. 55:9 / PROV. 3:19

Creation

In the beginning, God created the universe. He made the world and everything in it. He created humans in His own image to be His representatives on the earth.

Fall

The first humans, Adam and Eve, disobeyed God by eating from the fruit of the Tree of Knowledge of Good and Evil. Because of sin, the world was cursed. The punishment for sin is death, and because of Adam's original sin, all humans are sinful and condemned to death.

Redemption

God sent his Son to become a human and redeem His people. Jesus Christ lived a sinless life but died on the cross to pay the penalty for sin. He resurrected from the dead and ascended into heaven. All who put their faith in Jesus are saved from death and freely receive the gift of eternal life.

Restoration

One day, Jesus Christ will return again and restore all that sin destroyed. He will usher in a new heaven and new earth where all who trust in Him will live eternally with glorified bodies in the presence of God.

TIMELINE OF SCRIPTURE

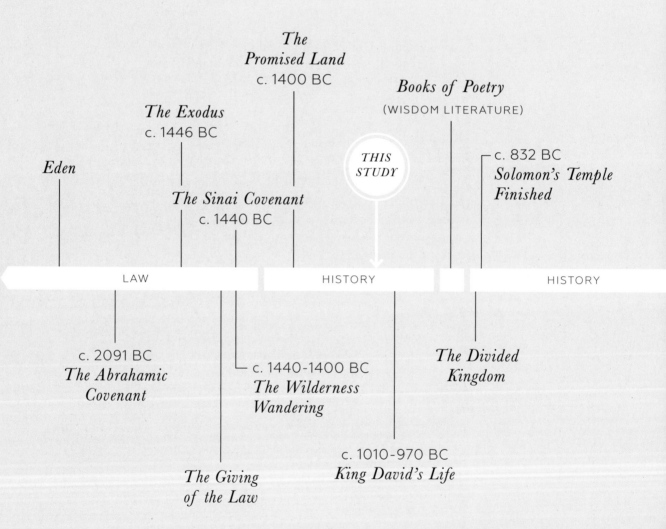

Eden

The Exodus
c. 1446 BC

The Sinai Covenant
c. 1440 BC

The
Promised Land
c. 1400 BC

Books of Poetry
(WISDOM LITERATURE)

THIS
STUDY

c. 832 BC
Solomon's Temple
Finished

LAW   HISTORY   HISTORY

c. 2091 BC
The Abrahamic
Covenant

c. 1440-1400 BC
The Wilderness
Wandering

The Divided
Kingdom

c. 1010-970 BC
King David's Life

The Giving
of the Law

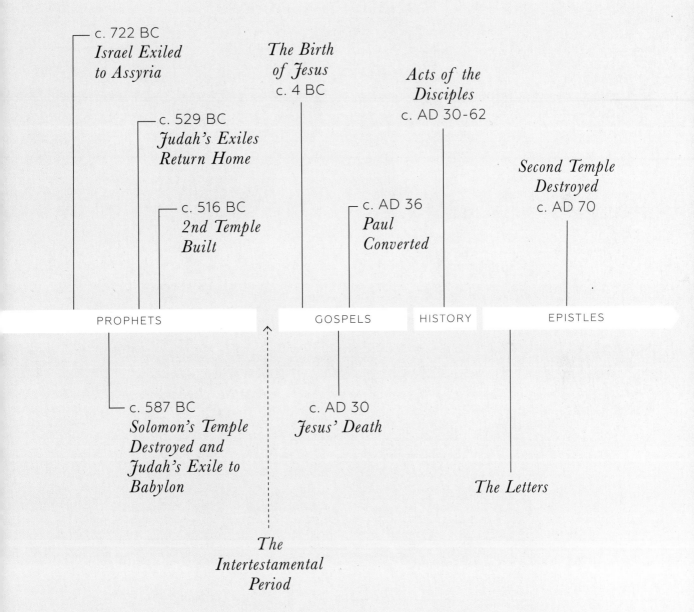

c. 722 BC
*Israel Exiled
to Assyria*

*The Birth
of Jesus*
c. 4 BC

*Acts of the
Disciples*
c. AD 30-62

c. 529 BC
*Judah's Exiles
Return Home*

*Second Temple
Destroyed*
c. AD 70

c. 516 BC
*2nd Temple
Built*

c. AD 36
*Paul
Converted*

PROPHETS   GOSPELS   HISTORY   EPISTLES

c. 587 BC
*Solomon's Temple
Destroyed and
Judah's Exile to
Babylon*

c. AD 30
Jesus' Death

The Letters

*The
Intertestamental
Period*

Table of
Contents

FIELDS OF GRACE

INTRODUCTION & EXTRAS

WEEK 1

WEEK 2

WEEK 3

WEEK 4

"
God works supernaturally through the simple faith of ordinary people.
"

INTRODUCTION

Read the entire book of Ruth

I flipped past the book of Ruth three times as I opened my Bible to begin this study. It is a tiny book tucked into the Old Testament that would be easy to miss among other bigger and perhaps seemingly more important books. Though this small book of Ruth may be short in length, it bears significant weight in its message. There is a fascination with the book of Ruth. We love stories, and we identify and admire the character of this book which draws many people in. It is interesting to note that the book of Ruth is the only Old Testament book named after a non-Israelite. It is also interesting to know that the book of Ruth was often read immediately after Proverbs 31 during Jewish feasts. Many scholars believe that the description of the Proverbs 31 woman was a description of Ruth. Ruth was certainly highly regarded as a woman of virtue, and we would be wise to imitate her character.

The book of Ruth is more than the story of a strong woman of virtue, though it is that. It is a love story but not just a love story of Ruth and Boaz—it is the love story of a God who was sovereignly and providentially laying each piece of the story of redemption into place. It is the story of God pursuing and redeeming His people. So the book of Ruth is not really about Ruth and Boaz—it is about God. We are left in awe, not of Ruth and Boaz but of the God of Ruth and Boaz. The book of Ruth reminds us that God works supernaturally through the simple faith of ordinary people. The book is about God using even the most difficult circumstances for the good of His people. And if God could do that for Ruth, He can certainly do it for you. God's providential grace is the unseen character of the book of Ruth. Ruth reminds us that God is always at work behind the scenes, even when His hand is not plainly seen. The

book of Ruth is a sweet glimpse at who God is and how He works. As we read of His sovereignty and faithfulness, we can hear Him telling us that this is who He is and that we can trust Him. Our sovereign Redeemer will be faithful to us.

Take time to read through the entire book of Ruth. Read it several times if you are able. Get a grasp on this story, and then let us dig deeper into this beautiful story.

"

The book of Ruth is a sweet glimpse at who God is and how He works.

"

NOTES

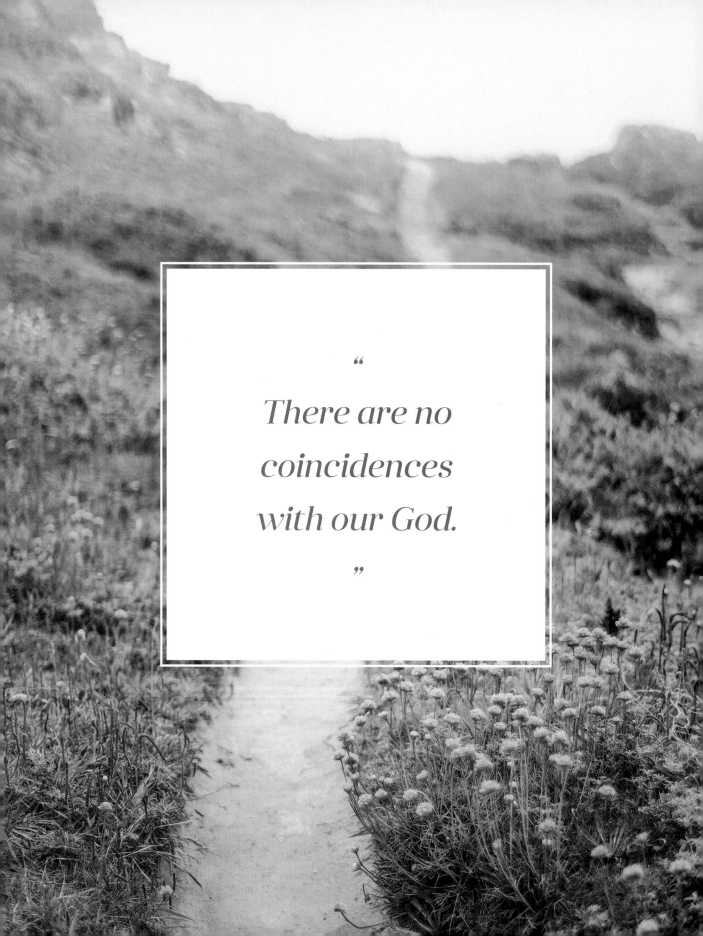

"
There are no coincidences with our God.
"

FAITHFUL GOD

Read Ruth 1:1

The book of Ruth opens with, "In the days when the judges ruled..." and by doing so, it places itself on the timeline of Scripture for us. Ruth is a story of redemption from a difficult time in the history of God's people. There was no king, and the people did what was right in their own eyes, as Judges 21:25 reminds us. And if the people were doing what was right in their own eyes, that usually meant that they were not doing what was right. Though God had been ever faithful, the people had been unfaithful. The people of Israel had slipped further and further into disobedience. What had started as complacency had turned into rebellious hearts. Sin is a slippery slope, and once we compromise a little, we soon find it hard to stand. Yet even when things were bad, God was at work. And even when it seemed that all had abandoned the Lord, there were a few who were faithful. We are told that there was a famine in the land, and this famine was likely the result of the people's disobedience (Deuteronomy 11:13-17). Bethlehem was known as the House of Bread, but this famine meant that there was not any bread in the House of Bread.

We are introduced to one man of Bethlehem who decided to take his family to greener pastures. The grass seemed greener in Moab—except it was not. Going to Moab meant leaving the Promised Land and going back into the wilderness from which God's people had been delivered. Moab was a wicked land, and God's people knew that. But it seems this man would follow the path of the people in the time of the judges and do what was right in his own eyes. The text uses the word "sojourn" for the man's journey to Moab which implies that he intended to be there temporarily. He intended to be there for a short time and then return to Bethlehem, but he would never return. So often we do the same. We

think we can leave the promised land where God has us and return shortly. We think maybe we know what is best for our lives. We think that maybe God's ways are not the best ways, but they always are. Yet even still, God was providentially working. Sinclair Ferguson reminds us that even the town was significant when he said, "It is not insignificant that all this takes place when 'there was no king in Israel' (Judges 21:25), yet in the very town where Israel's greatest king would later be reared (1 Samuel 16:1) and where the King of Kings would be born (Micah 5:2; Matthew 2:1)." There are no coincidences with our God. He is working even when we do not understand, and He can transform our greatest mistakes into the greatest of miracles. He is the faithful God.

"He is working even when we do not understand, and He can transform our greatest mistakes into the greatest of miracles."

In what ways are we tempted to do things our own way instead of trusting the Lord?

From seeking unwise council, listening to
our mind first instead of God's wisdom
we are tempted when we haven't been
in frequent + consistent contact with
God

What is a way that you have seen God bring good from a bad decision or situation in your life?

From the first guy I dated. Learned
what it truly meant to be equally
yoked, and this influenced positively
the people I want to date now. God
used that relationship to show me the
true man he has for me.

What situation in your life can you trust God to bring good from right now?

My singleness, I know it has a purpose, but
it can be tough to dwell in it and not
hope/want a relationship now

I've seen Him work all things for
good

"

We will all face difficulties, but how we react to them is so important.

"

RETURN

Read Ruth 1:2-6

The opening verses of the book are painting a picture for us. Elimelech and Naomi along with their two sons faced trying circumstances, and this family fled the land of promise to go to forbidden territory. They wanted the blessings of God, but they did not want to do things God's way. So often we can be the same way. We will all face difficulties, but how we react to them is so important. When we respond poorly to adversity, we can often make the situation worse. The family who in verse 1 had planned to sojourn, we now see in verse 2 remaining in Moab. They became comfortable outside of God's design. For Naomi, the situation grew bleak. We are not told of her role in going to Moab. Did she agree it was a good idea? Did she resist? Did she pray? We do not know for sure, but we watch on as Elimelech dies. And then just ten years later, her sons, Mahlon and Chilion, die as well. The situation looked dismal, but God was sovereignly working. To society, Naomi was hopeless, as widows were seen as the very bottom of the social strata. With no husband and no children to care for her, she was nearly helpless in this male-dominated society.

From man's perspective, Naomi was hopeless, but God saw every affliction she had faced. He saw her. He knew what was a result of her own poor choices and what was a result of the circumstances of her life, and through it all, He sovereignly had a plan for her good. As a loving Father, God was calling her to return and to come home. He was calling her home to Bethlehem but most of all, home to her God. The book of Ruth, and specifically this first chapter, is full of the Hebrew word *shuwb*, and it means to return, to restore, to revive. It points to God's covenant grace in calling His people back to Him. *Shuwb* is used in Psalm 19:7 and is translated as revive, and in Psalm 23:3, it is translated as restore. This

return has spiritual implications. It is a return to God's grace, and in so many ways we need to return to His grace every day and find restoration, revival, and refreshment in His Word. His kindness is meant to lead us to repentance (Romans 2:4). Naomi was right in the middle of the fields of Moab when she heard of God's faithfulness to His people in visiting them and giving them bread. Though she was in the middle of a foreign land and far from where she should have been, God was calling her and drawing her to Himself. How thankful we should be that He does the same for us. We have never wandered too far that He does not seek to draw us back to the promised land of His love and grace. He calls us to return and to be restored by who He is. In what ways is it easy for us to get comfortable outside of God's plan?

"We have never wandered too far that He does not seek to draw us back to the promised land of His love and grace."

Look up Psalm 23:3 and Psalm 19:7 where the Hebrew word *shuwb* is translated as restore and revive. Write down any observations you notice in these cross-references.

_____

_____

_____

_____

_____

_____

_____

What has God used in your life to restore and revive your heart?

_____

_____

_____

_____

_____

_____

_____

_____

How do we practically return to God's grace each day?

_____

_____

_____

_____

_____

_____

_____

_____

"
His love is powerful and strong and able to redeem anyone.
"

COVENANT LOVE

Read Ruth 1:7-14

Naomi has now heard of God visiting His people and giving food after the famine. She has decided to return to Bethlehem and to her God. Orpah and Ruth are determined to go with her, but Naomi pleads with them to stay. She wants them to have a good life, and staying would be the easier choice. Naomi asks God to deal kindly with them, and here we find the Hebrew word *Hesed*. This is God's rich covenant love for His people. It is His steadfast love, mercy, and grace poured out on His people. Naomi's use of the word in reference to women who were not Israelites is peculiar and powerful. She knew that God could pour out His grace on these women, even though they were not Israelites. His love is powerful and strong and able to redeem anyone. Staying in Moab seemed like the easier choice, and Naomi was well aware of all that came along with being a woman in a foreign land. Orpah would make the sensible choice and decide to stay. She chose logic over love and followed the wisdom of the world as she returned to her family and the land of Moab. But verse 14 tells us that Ruth clung to Naomi. This is speaking of covenant commitment, and the Hebrew word is the same word used to describe the marriage commitment in Genesis 2:24. The word is also used in the relationship of Israel to God, such as in Deuteronomy 13:4 in the context of God's people holding fast to Him. Ruth was committed to Naomi, and soon we will see that she was committed to Yahweh as well.

This life is full of choices. We can follow God to the unknown, or we can follow ourselves and the world's wisdom without Him. Following the world may seem like the easier choice, but it never is in the long run. Naomi pleaded that she had no son for them to marry and then proclaimed that God's hand had gone out against her. Naomi wanted

God to *hesed* Orpah and Ruth, but it seems that she feared that He would not *hesed* her. Yet His everlasting love reached right to her in the fields of Moab. We have never run too far that His *hesed* love does not call us to return. Naomi could not see past her circumstances and her past, and she had no idea that God was already working for her good. God is not against us—He is for us. Our circumstances may cloud our ability to see that, but we can cling to that truth. God would use even her mistakes for her good. We must remember as we read Scripture that these are real people with real emotions facing real circumstances with a very real God. Naomi faced both faith and doubt in her life. She was a real person just like us, and her God would prove real in her situation.

So will we follow God to the unknown? Will we trust that His way is best? We can rest secure in His steadfast love and know that His *hesed* love will never let us go.

"God is not against us – He is for us. Our circumstances may cloud our ability to see that, but we can cling to that truth."

What choices sometimes feel easier than following God?

_____

_____

_____

_____

_____

_____

In what area of life are you choosing today to trust God?

_____

_____

_____

_____

_____

_____

_____

_____

How have you seen God's steadfast love in your life?

_____

_____

_____

_____

_____

_____

_____

_____

> "
> *In Jesus we have
> been brought near.*
> "

THE LIFE OF FAITH

Read Ruth 1:15-18

Though Orpah made the more logical decision, Ruth was determined to follow Naomi, but we will learn that this was more than just loyalty to Naomi. It was also loyalty to the Lord. The language that Ruth uses is covenant language. It mimics the covenant language of Genesis 17:7-8 and Exodus 6:7. God had promised to Israel that He would be their God, and they would be His people. This leads us to believe that Ruth had some knowledge of the Scriptures and of the faithful love that God had for His people. This is the language of conversion. It was not just a commitment to Naomi, though that was certainly part of it. This is a commitment to God Himself. This is Ruth saying that though she was physically born a Moabite, she is now spiritually an Israelite. The conversion of Ruth has several similarities to the conversion of Rahab in Joshua 2, as we see foreign women who placed their faith in the grace and *hesed* love of God. Interestingly enough, Boaz is the son of Rahab. Perhaps Boaz saw a little of his own mother in the foreign, young woman who would come into his life. The book of Ruth is also a beautiful reminder of God's desire to draw all nations to Himself. Those of us who have trusted by faith in God's saving grace are now spiritually a part of God's chosen people as well. Galatians will tell us that in Christ we become heirs of Abraham and that in Jesus there is no Jew or Greek, slave or free, male or female (Galatians 3:7-9, 3:28-29). We were once far from God, but in Jesus we have been brought near, and we find peace in who He is (Ephesians 2:13-14). He Himself is our peace.

We are reminded that no matter how bad things seem to be, God is always drawing people to Himself. It was a dark time for Israel during the days of the judges, but even then, even when no one else could see it,

God was at work. He was calling a remnant to Himself and calling His people from all nations. This passage reminds us that our faith should be alive, and it should cause us to act. Faith in God causes us to act in faith! Faith impacts our everyday. Faith dictates our decisions. Faith changes the course of our lives. Faith gives us confidence under pressure and enables us to trust God against all odds. We must remember that this faith is not just wishful thinking, good vibes, or inspirational words. This is faith in the God who is working for us in all situations and who has promised everything for our good (Romans 8:28). Ruth chose in faith to follow the Lord, not knowing what the outcome would be. We must do the same with utter confidence that He will be faithful to us. When we choose to trust Him, our lives put the faithfulness of God on display. Whatever it is we are facing, we know that we can trust Him.

"When we choose to trust Him, our lives put the faithfulness of God on display."

DAY 5 QUESTIONS

How does knowledge of God's Word increase our faith?

How does our faith spur us to action?

How does faith enable us to trust the Lord?

BUT RUTH REPLIED:
DON'T PLEAD WITH ME TO
ABANDON YOU OR TO RETURN
AND NOT FOLLOW YOU.
FOR WHEREVER YOU GO,
I WILL GO, AND WHEREVER
YOU LIVE, I WILL LIVE;
YOUR PEOPLE WILL BE
MY PEOPLE, AND YOUR GOD
WILL BE MY GOD.

RUTH 1:16

WEEK *one* REFLECTION

Paraphrase the passage from this week.

What did you observe from this week's text about God and His character?

What does this week's passage reveal about the condition of mankind and about yourself?

How does this passage point to the gospel?

How should you respond to this passage? What is the personal application?

What specific action steps can you take this week to apply this passage?

> "
> *God had emptied*
> *her so that He*
> *could fill her.*
> "

FILL US LORD

Read Ruth 1:19-22

Ruth poured out her heart in beautiful covenant commitment, and Naomi's response was silence. Her heart was too jaded by her circumstances to see God's abundant faithfulness to her. We often have this same attitude asking, "Why me?" and some days we allow our hearts to grow so bitter that it seems impossible to shake this bad mood. But Naomi's story is one of God's faithfulness. When we allow bitterness and pride to overtake our hearts, our perception is easily skewed. Naomi claims that she went away full, and it seems that she had forgotten that she had fled from famine. She now feels, with short-sighted vision, that God had brought her back empty. What she failed to see was that she had left full of herself, and God had emptied her so that He could fill her. It is worth taking note that the chapter began with a famine and ends with a harvest. This timing was certainly part of God's sovereign plan and providence. The harvest would not just be physical but spiritual as well.

Unfortunately, Naomi was too blinded by herself to see the great harvest ahead. Naomi's name means pleasant, but as she returns to Bethlehem she asks to be called *Mara* which means bitter. *Mara* had a deeper significance for the people of Israel. After God had faithfully delivered his people in Exodus 14 through the Red Sea, they came to *Mara* where the water was bitter in Exodus 15:23- 25, and they grumbled and complained. Just like Naomi, they had forgotten that God is faithful and that we can always trust Him, even when our situation does not make sense. Bitterness prevents us from seeing how God is working. Naomi could not see the faithfulness of God because she was consumed by her past. She allowed herself to be defined by her circumstances instead of by her Creator. God was faithfully working though Naomi could not see with her

human eyes all that He was doing. So often we hold on to things that we think will bring us happiness, when the truth is that true joy is found only in Him. Naomi needed to learn what many of us do as well, as Martha Snell Nicholson said, "That God could not pour His riches into hands already full." Naomi had tried trusting herself, but things had not worked out the way that she had planned. God had emptied her hands, but He would soon fill them with the greatest blessings she could ever desire. Will we trust Him to do the same for us?

Lord, give us eyes to see that You are working.
Help us to trust You even when life does not make sense.
Empty us of ourselves, and fill us with You.

"Bitterness prevents us from seeing how God is working."

How can you have a biblical response to a "why me?" attitude?

How can we be blinded by ourselves and miss out on what God is doing?

What do you need to empty your heart of and lay down at His feet today?

"
*God is working
even when we
cannot clearly see
His sovereign hand.*
"

PROVIDENCE

Read Ruth 2:1-3

In so many ways, the book of Ruth is about divine providence. It reminds us that God is working even when we cannot clearly see His sovereign hand. These first three verses of chapter 2 give us a glimpse at what just so happened, or "as luck would have it." But we know that with God things do not just happen, and that as His people, we have no need to depend on luck. We do not always know His plans, and sometimes we may feel confused at the course of our life, but He is always working for our good (Romans 8:28). We do not need to know what God is doing to know that He is doing something.

Ruth and Naomi came back to Bethlehem with nothing, but back in Leviticus 19:9-10, God had provided a way for the poor and sojourners to work for food by gleaning in the fields of Israel. God had been so generous with His people, and He called them to be generous as well and to demonstrate His *hesed* love to others. In the time of the judges when men did what was right in their own eyes, we see that Boaz was a man of honor and character. The Hebrew word that describes him can even be translated as virtuous. Ruth was thought of as the example of a Proverbs 31 virtuous woman, and Boaz is described as a virtuous man. Even in hard times, Ruth did not sit home and sulk. She went to work. She did what she could and trusted that God would show up for her. In verse 2, she tells Naomi that she hoped to find favor. The Hebrew here is *chen*, and it is closely related to *hesed*. *Chen* is most often translated as grace. It was by God's sovereign grace that Ruth would find grace in the eyes of Boaz. We must be careful not to over romanticize this story or let our familiarity skew our view. Ruth did not go to that field thinking that she would find a husband. She went there unsure, hungry, and in a foreign

land. She did not know what was to come, but she knew the One who did. She simply did what she could. She was faithful to God in the small, everyday tasks and trusted that He would be faithful to her.

God's greatest work is often done in the bleakest of situations. We see that here in Ruth, and we need not look any further than the cross to see that Jesus died for us while we were yet sinners (Romans 5:8). The darkest night of the crucifixion brought forth the bright light of redemption. We can trust Him in our situations as well. We might not know what He is doing, but we can be sure that He is working for us. We might not know what the future holds, but we can know that the One who holds the future is holding us.

"We might not know what the future holds, but we can know that the One who holds the future is holding us."

How have you seen the providence of God in your life?

In what small daily tasks can you be faithful?

How is the gospel the ultimate example of good coming from bad because of God's grace?

"
*God would see
her faith and
not her past.*
"

GRACE UPON GRACE

Read Ruth 2:4-10

Ruth was diligently working in the fields when Boaz arrived on the scene. Immediately, we are struck by the character of Boaz who greets his workers in the name of the Lord. Boaz inquires about Ruth and is told that she is a Moabite woman who had come with Naomi back to Bethlehem and had asked to glean in the field. Boaz then speaks directly to Ruth. He does not call her a foreigner or a Moabite as others had. Instead, he speaks to her as a person and honors her dignity by calling her "my daughter." He did not identify her by her past. Perhaps Boaz had a special sympathy for Ruth who was a foreign woman who had placed her faith in Yahweh. Boaz's mother was a woman by the name of Rahab. We learn of her in the beginning chapter of the book of Joshua. Rahab had once been a prostitute, but she placed her faith in the God of Israel. God would see her faith and not her past. She called on God's *hesed* love to meet her in her sin, and she became a part of God's people by faith. When the walls of Jericho fell, Rahab and her family were saved. That same Rahab is the mother of Boaz.

In this unfolding story we will begin to see that Boaz is a picture, or a type, of Jesus. We will see this picture of Jesus right from our first interaction. Jesus makes outcasts daughters. He does not identify us by our past but gives us a new identity in Himself. This encounter with Boaz is likely the first ray of hope in this foreign land for Ruth. Boaz would bestow dignity and honor on Ruth by calling her to eat and drink freely and by protecting her in commanding the men not to touch her. Boaz showed favor to her. He showed her grace and the *hesed* love that had been shown to him by God. Boaz's treatment of Ruth is a beautiful picture of who Jesus is to us. Jesus calls us to eat at His table and drink the water of life

freely (John 6:35). Jesus brings beauty from our brokenness. Jesus gives us dignity. Jesus is our protector. He takes us in as foreigners who are slaves to sin and makes us daughters of God. Jesus makes us His own by His extravagant grace. In the fields of Boaz, Ruth would come poor and hungry, but she would leave with more than enough. Jesus is more than enough for us. We need only to look to the cross to see His love and grace on display. Boaz was a demonstrator of the grace of God to Ruth, and we have the opportunity to demonstrate God's grace to those around us as well. Our lives can point the world around us to the grace that only He gives—grace that is more than enough for every moment of every day.

"Our lives can point the world around us to the grace that only He gives."

Jesus gives us a new identity. In what things are we tempted to find our identity?

Because of how God has shown His love and grace to you,
how can you show love and grace to others?

Jesus is more than enough for us. List some things that Jesus is better than.

"

*God is the
shelter and security
of His children.*

"

SHALOM

Read Ruth 2:11-16

When Ruth questioned the grace and favor that Boaz was showing her, he responded to her with grace. He had heard of her character and all that she had done for Naomi. He did not view her as a foreigner because she was a woman who had been converted. He spoke to her as a daughter of Israel. Back in verse 8, he had told her to keep close to his young women. This is the same Hebrew word that was used in Ruth 1:14 as clung, and which denoted covenant commitment. Boaz was telling her, "You are one of us now." By her faith in the Lord, she had become part of the covenant community. Boaz prayed beautiful words for Ruth as he recognized her as no longer an outsider. He asked the Lord to repay, or give a full reward, to her for what she had done. This was not a prosperity gospel. It was not that God was in her debt. It was so much more beautiful than that. The Hebrew word for repay and full reward is *shalem* from the same root as *shalom*. This word had special meaning to God's people. *Shalom* means peace, wholeness, and completeness. This would not be found in things or in physical provision but in the provider Himself. This is the blessing of the covenant, or as Paul described in Ephesians 1:7, "the riches of his grace." This is what we have because of Jesus.

One of the most beautiful pictures in Scripture is of us coming under the wings of our God, and that is how Boaz describes Ruth. He says that she had found refuge under the wings of Yahweh. This imagery is used throughout the Psalms (Psalm 17:7-8, 36:7, 57:1, 61:4, 91:4), and it shows that God is the shelter and security of His children. This also pulls our memory back to the ark of the covenant and the wings that sheltered the mercy seat. It is the cross itself with its outstretched arms that points us to the outstretched arms of our merciful God.

We find refuge in the mercy of our God, sheltered under His almighty wings. Ruth's life had not been easy, but God would carry her through. Boaz speaks of the God of Israel as her God, again showing that she was no longer an outcast. Ruth was invited to eat and drink her fill. Ruth had come empty, but she would leave full. The same is true for us. We come to Jesus empty, with nothing to offer, and in Him we are satisfied. We find *shalom* in Jesus. We can trust Him. We can trust Him to provide for our daily needs and to provide peace for our souls. He works in ways we cannot see. Jesus is our *shalom*.

"

We come to Jesus empty, with nothing to offer, and in Him we are satisfied.

"

How do we find *shalom* peace in Jesus?

What have you found refuge from?

We come to Jesus with nothing, and He fills us.
List some things that Jesus fills us with.

> "
> *The solution to our own bitterness is to see God's steadfast love for us.*
> "

HESED

Read Ruth 2:17-20

Ruth gleaned in the field of Boaz until evening, and she returned home to Naomi with a whole lot of barley and leftover food from her meal with Boaz. It seems Naomi was anxious to hear what had happened and why Ruth was returning with such a bounty. Naomi's questions were coming at a rapid-fire before Ruth could even have time to answer. Certainly something had happened that day, and Naomi wanted to know! Ruth told her all that had happened, and Naomi's heart appears to soften, not only toward her situation but to the Lord as well.

Naomi speaks of Boaz when she says, "May he be blessed of the Lord." This blessing she speaks of is more than a shallow "#blessed" posted to social media. This blessing is God's favor and protection. This was not simply material blessing but the blessings that God is always working on behalf of His children. Then in Ruth 2:20 is the word "kindness," and this is where we see Naomi's heart soften as God's faithful love breaks down barriers of bitterness. She was beginning to recognize that through it all, God had been faithful. Kindness here is *hesed*—the covenant, faithful, and steadfast love of God. The kindness Boaz showed Ruth was really the *hesed* love of God. Naomi's bitter heart began to melt as she began to see God working for her in faithfulness and steadfast *hesed* love. The solution to our own bitterness is to see God's steadfast love for us. We need to be reminded that He is for us and not against us—that His ways are so much higher than our own. The word *hesed* is found roughly 250 times in the Old Testament. It is a key word of the entire Old Testament and is one of the most frequent descriptors of the character of God. This is who God is. He is the God who pursues covenant with us—a covenant that is utterly dependent on Him. He is the God who loves us at our darkest and calls for us to return to Him.

Naomi was a woman who had wandered from God to the fields of Moab, and yet His faithful love pursued her even there. And even when her circumstances blinded her eyes, He was working in His covenant *hesed* love to bring something good from her life. We get just a glimpse as we see the realization that Boaz is a redeemer, and soon we will see all that God was doing.

There will be days when we do not know what He is doing. There will be days when we do not feel particularly blessed. Yet even then we can trust that He is working. With the eyes of faith we can look at our life and know that though in that moment we cannot see His hand in our situation, we know that He is there. We can trust Him in the turmoil because we know who He is. He is the God who showers us in *hesed* love, the love that we cannot find just one word to explain—His covenant, faithful, gracious, and merciful steadfast love. So we will choose to trust even when we cannot see!

"He is the God who loves us at our darkest and calls for us to return to Him."

What is a situation in your life that seemed bad in the moment,
and yet you saw God bring good from it?

_____

_____

_____

_____

_____

What are you tempted to grow bitter about, and how does
God's character remind you to trust Him?

_____

_____

_____

_____

_____

_____

How should the knowledge of God's love change your outlook on your situation?

_____

_____

_____

_____

_____

_____

HOW PRICELESS YOUR
FAITHFUL LOVE IS, GOD!
PEOPLE TAKE REFUGE IN THE
SHADOW OF YOUR WINGS.

PSALM 36:7

WEEK *Two* REFLECTION

REVIEW RUTH 1:19-2:20

Paraphrase the passage from this week.

What did you observe from this week's text about God and His character?

What does this week's passage reveal about the condition of mankind and about yourself?

How does this passage point to the gospel?

How should you respond to this passage? What is the personal application?

What specific action steps can you take this week to apply this passage?

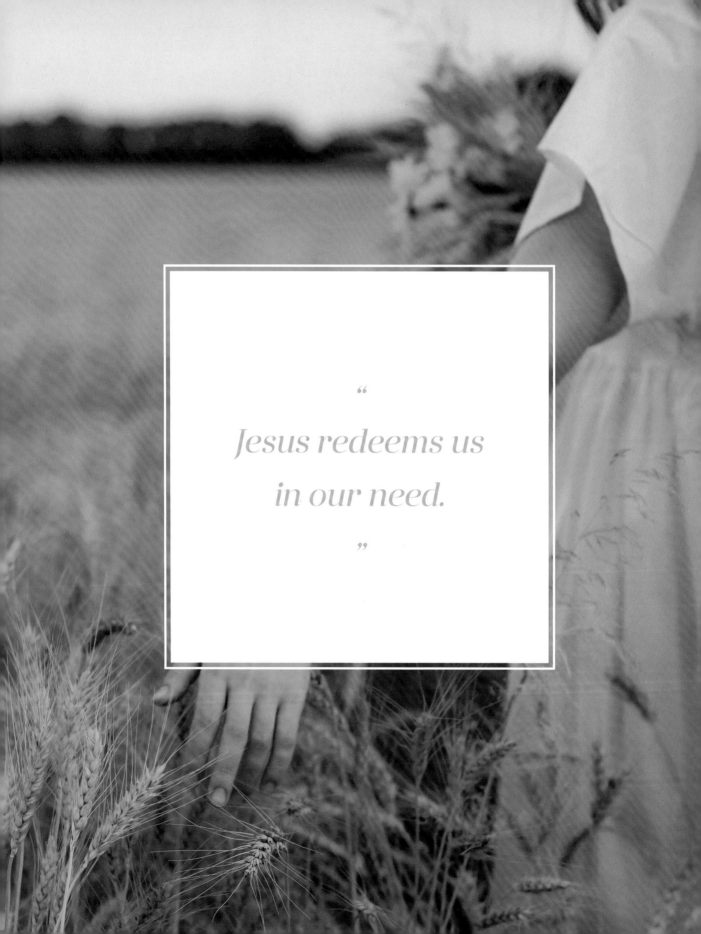

> "
> *Jesus redeems us*
> *in our need.*
> "

THERE IS A REDEEMER

Read Ruth 2:21-23

As Ruth returns from the field to Naomi, we see a glimpse of what is coming as Naomi recognizes that Boaz is a redeemer. In order to understand the significance of the redeemer, we must look back at the law. God had enacted a covenant with His people, and the Promised Land was one of the blessings of that covenant. Because God wanted to bless His people even in difficult circumstances, He made a system where families would help each other if someone fell on hard times. The land, though owned by God, was entrusted to the people as an inheritance. If a man died or was facing hard times, a *go'el* could help. *Go'el* is the Hebrew word translated as redeemer and often referred to as a kinsman-redeemer. Instructions for this role and situation were given in Leviticus 25:23-55 and Deuteronomy 25:5-10. *Go'els* redeemed those in need, and they protected the covenant from the impact of the fall.

As a widow, Ruth found herself in need of a redeemer, and Naomi recognized that Boaz might be the man. There is one other thing that the role of the *go'el* did. It pointed to Jesus. The *go'el* would redeem those in need, and Jesus redeems us in our need. The *go'el* was required to be a close relative, and in order to redeem us, Jesus became our close relative by becoming a man and at the cross, He became sin for us. A *go'el* had to pay a high price to redeem, and Jesus paid the price with His own blood for our redemption. The *go'el* also had to be willing—Jesus became a willing sacrifice for us. He did what He was not required to do. He became our *go'el* because He wanted us, just as the kinsman-redeemer protected the covenant people from the curse of the fall. Jesus redeems everything for our good, even the things from which it seems good could never come (Romans 8:28). We have an inheritance because of our Re-

deemer (Romans 8:16-17, Colossians 1:12, 1 Peter 1:3-4, Galatians 3:28-29, Ephesians 1:11). The Redeemer has the power to work any situation for our good. He can sovereignly and providentially direct history for the good of His people. Our great kinsman-redeemer will be faithful to us. Jesus redeems us in salvation, and He can also redeem our situations.

"

Jesus redeems everything for our good, even the things from which it seems good could never come.

"

What have you seen Him redeem in your life?

What aspect of Jesus as our *go'el* is the most meaningful to you? Why?

What is something that you have seen God sovereignly direct in your life?
What can you pray for His direction in now?

> "
> They had full
> confidence in the
> providence and
> sovereignty of God.
> "

REST AND REDEMPTION

Read Ruth 3:1-9

We have already seen Naomi's heart softening toward the Lord and even a glimpse of the promise of a redeemer in Ruth 2:20. Now the story continues to play out before us while pointing us to a much greater story. Our protagonist, Ruth, is a young widow in a foreign land. But she is also a young woman who has turned to Yahweh. In a culture where marriages were arranged more often than not, Naomi would have felt the weight of responsibility for the welfare of Ruth. Naomi was compelled to find rest or a home for Ruth. And though marriage and home are a beautiful concept here on earth, we must be careful to remember that our true home and rest are found in God alone. Nevertheless, Naomi knew that especially in this culture, marriage would make life much easier for Ruth. It would have been culturally unacceptable for Naomi to approach Boaz, so Naomi comes with another plan instead. The plan seems odd to us, but it is filled with significance. Though the plan was risky, it appears that Ruth and Naomi had confidence in the virtue and character of Boaz. But much more than that, they had full confidence in the providence and sovereignty of God.

Ruth came and lay down at the feet of Boaz as a sign of humility and submission. She also came to him in need and boldly asked for redemption. In this same way, we come to Christ needy and in need of a redeemer. We can come boldly and with confidence to the Lord because we know His character (Hebrews 4:16). Ezekiel 16:8 even gives us a picture of how God Himself spreads the corner of His garment over His children as He enters covenant with them. We can come boldly to God and ask Him to cover us in His unending grace and mercy.

Every part of Ruth's story points us to God Himself and the work of Jesus. We cannot help but notice that the wording of Ruth's request is similar to what Boaz said to her in chapter 2 — that she had taken refuge under the wings of Yahweh. We are again reminded of the spread wings of the angels over the mercy seat. Jesus will fulfill every promise to be the Redeemer for us, and Ruth's life is like a billboard pointing to the Messiah. Ruth is humbly and boldly asking for redemption, and it is a beautiful picture of how we come to our kinsman-redeemer as well. John Macarthur said, "Jesus is our true kinsman-redeemer, who becomes our human brother, buys us back from our bondage to evil, redeems our lives from death, and ultimately returns everything we have lost because of our sin." We come to our Savior boldly and humbly, believing in expectation that He will rescue us.

Marriage is meant to point us to the gospel, and this is no different. This book is meant to uncover the deeper story of how our God loves us, and that story is even better than the romance of Ruth and Boaz. We come to Jesus as destitute foreigners. We come in need of a Redeemer. We come to Him humbly and also with great boldness. And it is in Jesus that we find the kinsman-redeemer who gives us rest for our souls (Matthew 11:28). He is the one who covers us in His grace. We are covered under His almighty wings and covered with His kingly garment. He is our Redeemer, and we are His people.

"We come to our Savior boldly and humbly, believing in expectation that He will rescue us."

How have you found rest in God?

How should our relationship with God be thought of as both humble and bold?

Ruth's life pointed to Jesus. How can your life point to Him as well?

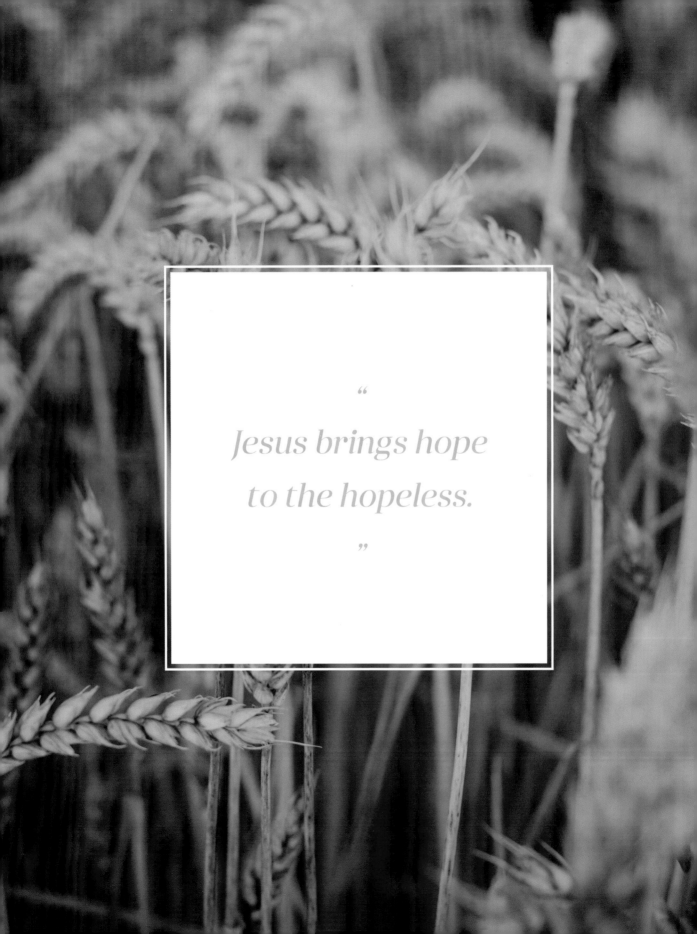

"
*Jesus brings hope
to the hopeless.*
"

A WOMAN OF VIRTUE

Read Ruth 3:10-13

In a beautiful picture of how we can come boldly in prayer, Ruth came to Boaz with her request. We can come boldly to the Lord with confidence that He will answer us. With the possibility of another kinsman, Boaz did not promise exactly how Ruth would be taken care of, but he promised that he would take care of her. Ruth was seeking after God's will by following the Lord. Boaz commended her that she did not just seek after the young men or riches. Ruth came hopeless, and Boaz gave her hope. We come to Jesus broken and hopeless, but Jesus brings hope to the hopeless. Ruth was a woman with a past, but Boaz would give her a future. Jesus does the same for us. Boaz speaks of Ruth's character and says that all of the townspeople know that she is a worthy, or a virtuous, woman. The word here for worthy or virtuous has been used to describe Boaz in Ruth 2:1, and it is the same word used to describe the Proverbs 31 woman. In the Hebrew Bible, the book of Ruth would have been found directly after Proverbs 31, and many Hebrew scholars believe that the woman described in Proverbs 31 is Ruth. The wording here for townsmen is literally translated "gates" and is the same word found in Proverbs 31:31 that speaks of the virtuous woman saying that her works praise her in the gates. This was certainly true of Ruth. Her character went before her. All of Bethlehem knew how she loved God and how she sacrificially loved Naomi.

As women, we have the power to influence the spiritual climate of our homes and those around us. What influence do we have? Do those around us know that we are women who love the Lord? Are we known for sacrificial love and service? Do people spend time with us and know that we have been with Jesus as was known of Peter and John in Acts 4:13? Do our faces and lives reflect the glory of God like Moses did in Exodus 34:29? We become like Jesus by spending time with Him. May we be known as His people. May our lives reflect His glory.

"

As women, we have the power to influence the spiritual climate of our homes and those around us.

"

What bold prayers does God want you to pray?

How would the people around you describe you? How do you want them to describe you?

How can you practically point those around you to Jesus?

"

God never leaves
His children empty.

"

HE IS WORKING IN THE WAITING

Read Ruth 3:14-18

Boaz would send Ruth back to Naomi in the early morning hours. But he would not send her back empty-handed. Boaz would send her back with six measures of barley which is an incredible amount. Some scholars have said this could have been upwards of eighty pounds. Her hands were certainly not empty as she returned to Naomi. It is interesting to note that the Hebrew word here in verse 17 for empty-handed is the same word used by Naomi in Ruth 1:21 when Naomi said that God had brought her back empty. How quick we are to think that we are empty or that we have been forgotten, but this is just another reminder that God never leaves His children empty. Our God is the one who fills His people with plentiful redemption and pours out His steadfast *hesed* love to us (Psalm 130:7). Not only does God not leave us empty, He also does not give us just enough to scrape by. He fills us to overflowing. He overwhelms us with His steadfast love and gives us plentiful redemption. In John 10:10, Jesus would explain that He did not only come to give us life but to give us abundant life. Naomi and Ruth were no longer empty, and we are no longer empty either. By His grace, we are no longer what we once were.

It is ironic to note how the once bitter Naomi has become a gospel teacher as she tells Ruth to wait and trust and see how the matter will turn out. Ruth could rest and wait because Boaz was at work for her. In the same way, we can wait and rest because the Lord is at work for us. We can be still and trust because our kinsman-redeemer is working for us. Our God can redeem anything, and we can trust Him to redeem our situations as well. This passage points us right to the gospel and what God has done for us. He has done what we could not do. Boaz sent Ruth with a mul-

titude of barley as a down-payment of sorts for the full redemption and restoration that was on the way. We have been given a down-payment as well. Ephesians 1:14 tells us that the Holy Spirit is the guarantee, or the down-payment, of our inheritance. This is the now aspect of our salvation. We live with just a glimpse of the full restoration and inheritance that will come someday because of what Jesus has done. He is our hope. He is our peace. He is our provider. He is working in our waiting and has given us Himself to walk through this life as a reminder that He will one day make all things new. So we look to the cross as assurance that He will provide (Romans 8:32). For now, we will trust Him in the waiting and praise Him for the plentiful redemption that He has lavished on us.

"For now, we will trust Him in the waiting and praise Him for the plentiful redemption that He has lavished on us."

What situations have you faced that can tempt you to think
you have been forgotten or left empty?

_____

_____

_____

_____

_____

_____

What are you waiting for right now?

_____

_____

_____

_____

_____

_____

How does the gospel enable you to trust God to provide?

_____

_____

_____

_____

_____

_____

_____

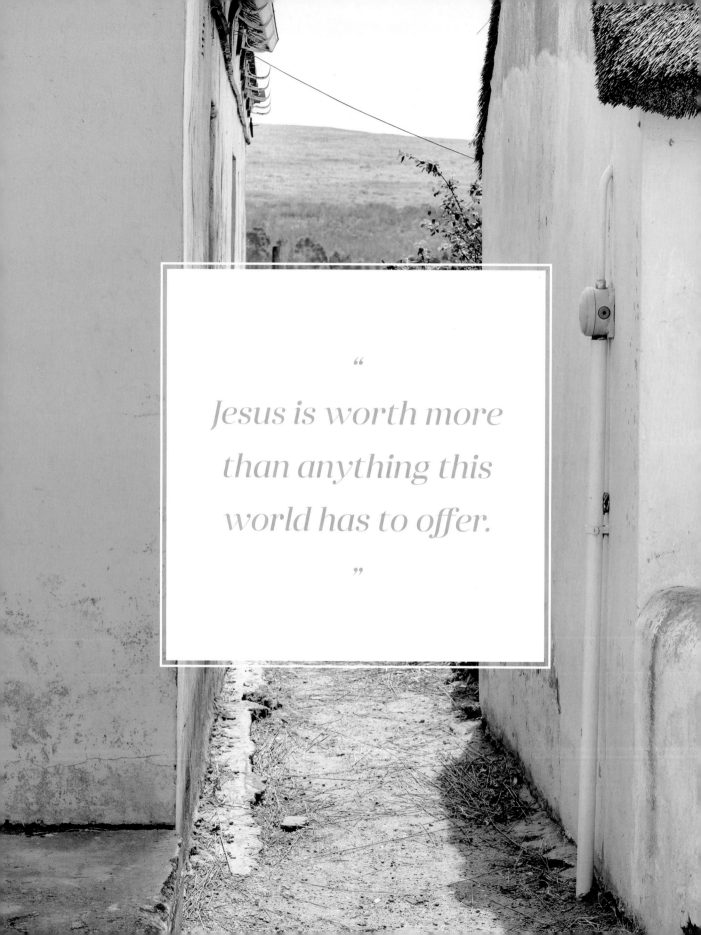

"

Jesus is worth more than anything this world has to offer.

"

WILLING TO REDEEM

Read Ruth 4:1-6

Just as Naomi had said, Boaz went right away to work for Ruth. Boaz was actively pursuing Ruth's redemption. Chapter 3 began with Naomi desiring rest for Ruth and ended with the assurance that Boaz would not rest until redemption was secured. Redemption was coming. Its promise was sure.

Verse 1 tells us that the other redeemer came by. The word "behold" shows us again the providence of our God who is always working behind the scenes. Nothing just so happens with our God. We meet this close redeemer who the Hebrew addresses literally as "Mr. So-and-So." At first, he is quick to agree to redeem. He is thinking it might be a shrewd business deal with the potential for great monetary gain. But as Boaz explains more, he backs out quickly. Taking on Ruth and Naomi would come at a great personal cost. It would require sacrifice and selfless love, but this near kinsman was only interested in selfish gain and selfishly thought only for himself. Boaz, as a picture of Jesus, thought for the good of Naomi and Ruth. So-and-So missed out on being a part of the story of redemption because he was self-focused instead of trusting God's design. And just like Orpah before him, we do not hear his name mentioned again.

Boaz was willing to be used by God. He was willing to pay the price. Dean Ulrich said, "Our faithfulness becomes the stage for God to per-form mighty deeds." God does not need us to fulfill His plans, and yet He invites us in. Boaz imaged Jesus who was willing to pay a high price for our redemption. We must remember that God's economy is different than ours. God works in ways that we do not understand. Jesus is worth more than anything this world has to offer.

Philippians 3:8 tells us that we can count everything else as loss because of the great worth of knowing Jesus. Following Jesus is always worth it. Ruth learned this truth as she left the familiarity of Moab to follow Yahweh, and we see this truth again as Boaz steps into God's grand plan of redemption by choosing to follow God. Boaz points us to Jesus again. We serve the One who was willing to redeem us. And now He is still willing to redeem any brokenness in our lives. We can bring our sin, our shame, and our brokenness to the cross. We can come to Him because He came to us.

"

We serve the One who was willing to redeem us. And now He is still willing to redeem any brokenness in our lives.

"

What is the cost of following Jesus?

Why is knowing Jesus better than anything else?

What has God redeemed in your life?

WE KNOW THAT ALL THINGS
WORK TOGETHER FOR THE GOOD
OF THOSE WHO LOVE GOD,
WHO ARE CALLED ACCORDING
TO HIS PURPOSE.

ROMANS 8:28

WEEK *Three* REFLECTION

Paraphrase the passage from this week.

_____

_____

_____

_____

_____

_____

_____

What did you observe from this week's text about God and His character?

_____

_____

_____

_____

_____

_____

_____

_____

What does this week's passage reveal about the condition of mankind and about yourself?

_____

_____

_____

_____

_____

_____

How does this passage point to the gospel?

_____

_____

_____

_____

_____

_____

_____

How should you respond to this passage? What is the personal application?

_____

_____

_____

_____

_____

_____

_____

What specific action steps can you take this week to apply this passage?

_____

_____

_____

_____

_____

_____

_____

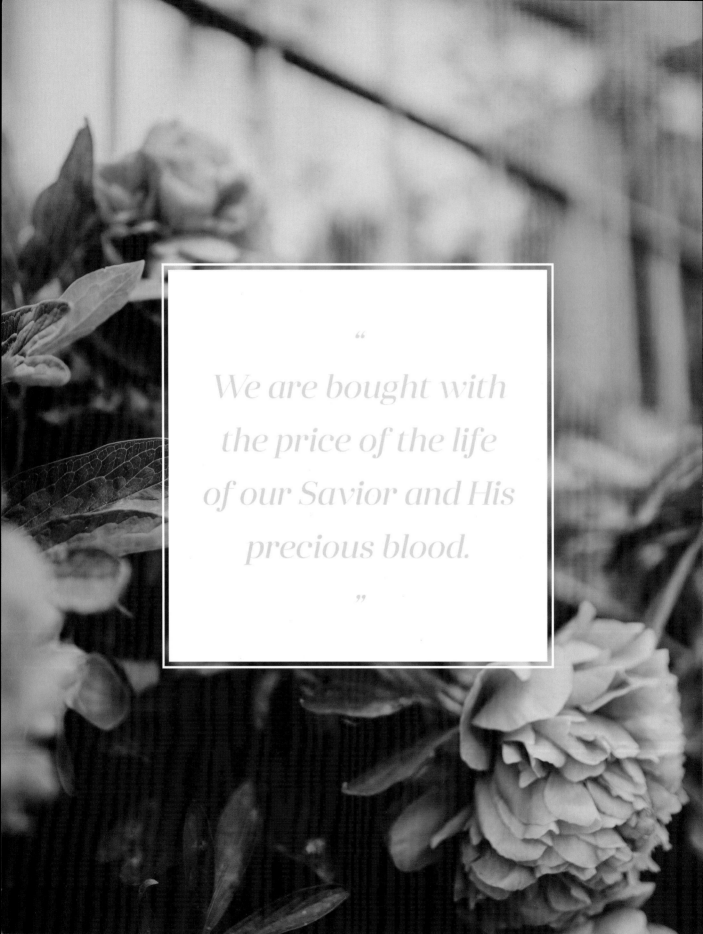

"

We are bought with
the price of the life
of our Savior and His
precious blood.

"

BOUGHT WITH A PRICE

Read Ruth 4:7-12

Boaz was willing to redeem. He was willing to pay the price to rescue Ruth. He joyfully paid the price though he had nothing to gain in this transaction. Ruth was bought with a price. 1 Corinthians 6:20 tells us that we also have been bought with a price. We are bought with the price of the life of our Savior and His precious blood. Boaz would take on the responsibility of caring for Ruth, and Jesus has taken on the responsibility of caring for us. We can rest in Him and find peace in Him because He will take care of us. The witnesses gathered around for this marriage ceremony in joy. Everyone loves a good love story, and this was a good one. Because this love story was pointing to the greatest love story of all time. The witnesses prayed that God would bless Ruth like He blessed Rachel and Leah, because it was through Rachel and Leah and their thirteen children that God would build the family of His chosen people. The people were praying that God would build Israel through Ruth — little did they know just how miraculously God would answer that prayer. The witnesses would also mention Tamar and Perez in their prayer. It certainly seems like an unlikely story of brokenness to remember, and yet it reminds us of how our God works through broken and sinful people to bring about His perfect plan. God uses unlikely people and unlikely circumstances to show His covenant faithfulness. He will surely do the same for us as well. God would answer the prayers of these witnesses in amazing ways.

We are seeing a picture of redemption as Boaz redeems Ruth from her hopeless situation, and soon we will see an even greater connection to our great Redeemer. The book of Ruth reminds us of the "already but not yet" of our redemption. Ruth would taste a glimpse of the coming

redemption through Boaz, and it would point to the redemption that Jesus would bring at the cross. The Old Testament constantly points us to the redemption for which the whole world was yearning. The people were awaiting the Messiah who would come and redeem, and the story of Ruth gives us a picture of that redemption. In Jesus, we are redeemed, and we await the full restoration that will come when Jesus returns and makes all things new. Because we have been bought with a price (1 Corinthians 6:20), we should praise our Redeemer and give our life to Him. Our redemption should propel us to praise. May we give everything to the One who gave everything for us.

"

God uses unlikely people and unlikely circumstances to show His covenant faithfulness. He will surely do the same for us as well.

"

How does the story of Ruth and Boaz point to the story of our redemption?

_____

_____

_____

_____

_____

How have you seen God's faithfulness in unlikely circumstances?

_____

_____

_____

_____

_____

_____

Jesus gave everything for us. What may He be asking you to give up to serve Him more?

_____

_____

_____

_____

_____

_____

"
Women found in God's Word faced delayed fulfillment of their desires.
"

A RESTORER OF LIFE

Read Ruth 4:13-16

Ruth and Boaz would marry as a beautiful picture of God's *hesed* love. And Yahweh would open Ruth's once barren womb and give her the conception of a son. Ruth had been married for ten years without being able to conceive, but now in God's sovereign timing, she would conceive a son. This miraculous conception was one of many miraculous conceptions in Scripture that pointed to the even more miraculous conception of Jesus to a young, virgin girl. These women found in God's Word faced delayed fulfillment of their desires. Sometimes God delays fulfilling our desires so that when He brings it to pass, we will know that it was Him. He is the one who makes the impossible possible, just as the angel declared to Mary about the birth of her own miracle baby in Luke 1:37. And He is also the one who walks with us every step of the way. The women of the town would praise God with Naomi because God had been faithful to her. What a different song now came from the woman who had once asked to be called Mara.

The child of Ruth and Boaz would also be a *go'el*, or a redeemer, for this family. He would care for Ruth and Naomi as they aged. He would meet their needs. We can pause to take notice that the child is described as a restorer of life. The Hebrew for restorer is the word *shuwb*, the same word we saw over and over in chapter 1. God had been lovingly calling Naomi to return to His grace and to find the restoration and refreshment that only He can give. Now He was showing that grace to her again. He was restoring her soul (Psalm 23:3). Her grandson would be a restorer and bring hope for the future. He would not erase the pain of the loss and grief that she had experienced, but he would bring fresh hope. Even our loss and our pain point us to Jesus and the hope and assurance that

we have in Him. In Him we can trust that one day all that has been lost will be restored. Naomi's hands were full as she held her young grandson, and her heart was full as she saw God's faithfulness through it all. Her life had not been easy, but her God had been faithful to her. And this baby boy who would grow to meet her needs and restore her life merely pointed to another baby boy born in miraculous circumstances in the same town of Bethlehem. Jesus is the one who meets our every need and restores our life. God is always faithful to His people, and we know that He will be faithful to us.

"Sometimes God delays fulfilling our desires so that when He brings it to pass, we will know that it was Him."

Can you remember instances in Scripture or in your own life where God did the impossible?

_____

_____

_____

_____

_____

_____

What should our response be to God's faithfulness?

_____

_____

_____

_____

_____

_____

_____

_____

How does the promise of restoration give you hope?

_____

_____

_____

_____

_____

_____

_____

_____

"

We have been redeemed into the family of God.

"

FROM GRIEF TO GRACE

Read Ruth 4:17-22

As we come to the end of our study of the book of Ruth, we may feel disappointed that the book closes with a genealogy. Most of us have been tempted at times to skim over these lists of names in Scripture. Yet it is in this closing genealogy that we find the greatest part of the story. It is here in these final verses that we learn just how this story will end. It is here that we learn that Boaz fathers Obed, and Obed fathers Jesse, and Jesse fathers David. Yes, Ruth would be the great grandmother of King David. And yet the story gets even better than that. Ruth's name is found in another very important genealogy in Matthew 1. It is there that we find her name in the genealogy of none other than Jesus. Ruth who was a foreigner, who lived a broken life, and whose life pointed to the redemption of Jesus would also be named in His family tree. God would take this foreign Moabite woman who started far from God and bring her near (Ephesians 2:13). And then He would bring the Messiah through her.

The book of Ruth points us to our own redemption. We see the hopeless condition of Naomi and Ruth, and we are reminded of our own hopeless condition. We see the Redeemer willing to do what it takes and pay an exceedingly high price, and we are reminded of Jesus who paid for our redemption with His own life. Jesus is our *go'el* who recognizes our hopeless condition and comes to our rescue. We have been redeemed from sin and death, and we have been redeemed into the family of God. The story of Ruth also reminds us that God is sovereignly working in ways that we cannot see. He is always working for the good of His people (Romans 8:28). God's grace can redeem any person and any situation.

So no matter what situation life brings, we can trust that God can redeem anything. Ruth and Naomi certainly did not as they returned back to Bethlehem. We may not always understand His plan, but we can always trust Him.

The book of Ruth starts with no king in Israel and ends with the genealogy of the King of Kings. It begins with no bread and ends with the Bread of Life. It would be in those same fields of Boaz in that little town of Bethlehem many years later that history will tell us that the angels announced the birth of the true Redeemer as angels sang to shepherds and announced the birth of Jesus. God was faithful to provide for Ruth in those fields, and it would be there that the greatest provision of all time would be heralded. Jesus is both our provision and our provider. The book of Ruth is so much more than just a love story; it is a picture of the greatest love story of all time. Ruth is a story of covenant redemption. It is a reminder that God brings good out of our brokenness.

It is a story of poverty to provision, brokenness to beauty, reproach to redemption, famine to fullness, grief to grace. It is the story of the gospel.

"Jesus is both our provision and our provider."

List out some of the aspects of God's character that you observed
while studying the book of Ruth.

_____

_____

_____

_____

_____

_____

What aspect of God's character stood out to you most
in the study of the book of Ruth? Why?

_____

_____

_____

_____

_____

_____

_____

How can you view your own life circumstances differently in light of the book of Ruth?

_____

_____

_____

_____

_____

_____

_____

THE NEIGHBOR WOMEN SAID,
"A SON HAS BEEN BORN TO NAOMI,"
AND THEY NAMED HIM OBED.
HE WAS THE FATHER OF JESSE,
THE FATHER OF DAVID.

RUTH 4:17

WEEK *four* REFLECTION
REVIEW RUTH 4:7-22

Paraphrase the passage from this week.

_____

_____

_____

_____

_____

_____

What did you observe from this week's text about God and His character?

_____

_____

_____

_____

_____

_____

_____

What does this week's passage reveal about the condition of mankind and about yourself?

_____

_____

_____

_____

_____

_____

How does this passage point to the gospel?

How should you respond to this passage? What is the personal application?

What specific action steps can you take this week to apply this passage?

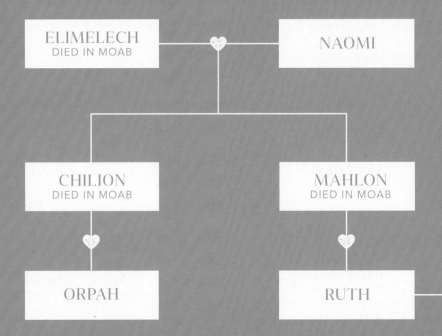

ELIMELECH
DIED IN MOAB

NAOMI

CHILION
DIED IN MOAB

MAHLON
DIED IN MOAB

ORPAH

RUTH

Ruth and the Genealogy of Jesus

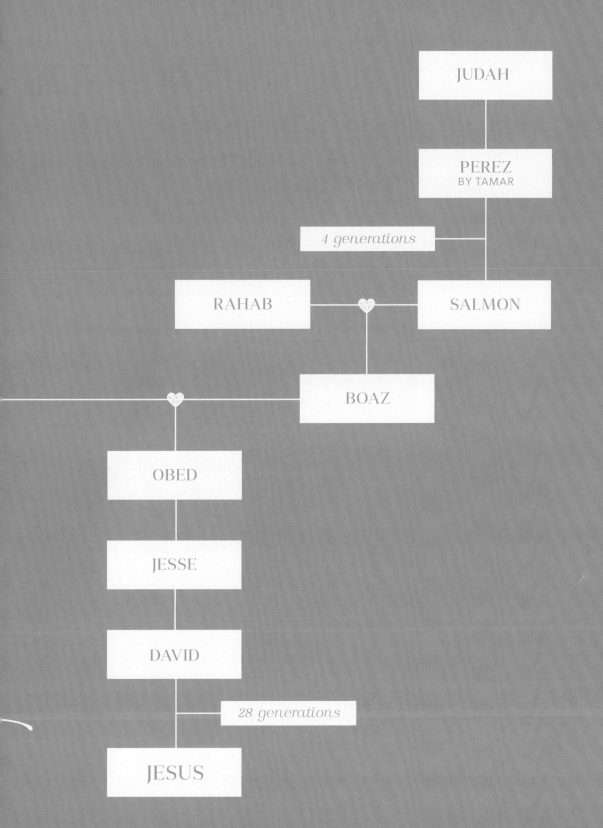

JUDAH

PEREZ
BY TAMAR

4 generations

RAHAB — SALMON

BOAZ

OBED

JESSE

DAVID

28 generations

JESUS

What is the Gospel?

THANK YOU FOR READING AND ENJOYING THIS STUDY WITH US! WE ARE ABUNDANTLY GRATEFUL FOR THE WORD OF GOD, THE INSTRUCTION WE GLEAN FROM IT, AND THE EVER-GROWING UNDERSTANDING ABOUT GOD'S CHARACTER FROM IT. WE ARE ALSO THANKFUL THAT SCRIPTURE CONTINUALLY POINTS TO ONE THING IN INNUMERABLE WAYS: THE GOSPEL.

We remember our brokenness when we read about the fall of Adam and Eve in the garden of Eden (Genesis 3), when sin entered into a perfect world and maimed it. We remember the necessity that something innocent must die to pay for our sin when we read about the atoning sacrifices in the Old Testament. We read that we have all sinned and fallen short of the glory of God (Romans 3:23) and that the penalty for our brokenness, the wages of our sin, is death (Romans 6:23). We all are in need of grace and mercy, but most importantly, we all need a Savior.

We consider the goodness of God when we realize that He did not plan to leave us in this dire state. We see His promise to buy us back from the clutches of sin and death in Genesis 3:15. And we see that promise accomplished with Jesus Christ on the cross. Jesus Christ knew no sin yet became sin so that we might become righteous through His sacrifice (2 Corinthians 5:21). Jesus was tempted in every way that we are and lived sinlessly. He was reviled yet still yielded Himself for our sake, that we may have life abundant in Him. Jesus lived the perfect life that we could not live and died the death that we deserved.

The gospel is profound yet simple. There are many mysteries in it that we can never exhaust this side of heaven, but there is still overwhelming weight to its implications in this life. The gospel is the telling of our sinfulness and God's goodness, and this gracious gift compels a response. We are saved by grace through faith, which means that we rest with faith in the grace that Jesus Christ displayed on the cross (Ephesians 2:8-9). We cannot save ourselves from our brokenness or do any amount of good works to merit God's favor, but we can have faith that what Jesus accomplished in His death, burial, and resurrection was more than enough for our salvation and our eternal delight. When we accept God, we are commanded to die to our self and our sinful desires and live a life worthy of the calling we have received (Ephesians 4:1). The gospel compels us to be sanctified, and in so doing, we are conformed to the likeness of Christ Himself. This is hope. This is redemption. This is the gospel.

SCRIPTURE TO REFERENCE:

GENESIS 3:15
I will put hostility between you and the woman, and between your offspring and her offspring. He will strike your head, and you will strike his heel.

ROMANS 3:23
For all have sinned and fall short of the glory of God.

ROMANS 6:23
For the wages of sin is death, but the gift of God is eternal life in Christ Jesus our Lord.

2 CORINTHIANS 5:21
He made the one who did not know sin to be sin for us, so that in him we might become the righteousness of God.

EPHESIANS 2:8-9
For you are saved by grace through faith, and this is not from yourselves; it is God's gift — not from works, so that no one can boast.

EPHESIANS 4:1
Therefore I, the prisoner in the Lord, urge you to walk worthy of the calling you have received,

Thank you for studying
God's Word with us!

CONNECT WITH US

@thedailygraceco

@kristinschmucker

CONTACT US

info@thedailygraceco.com

SHARE

#thedailygraceco

#lampandlight

VISIT US ONLINE

thedailygraceco.com

MORE DAILY GRACE

The Daily Grace App
Daily Grace Podcast